FIFA WORLD CUP SUPER STARS

FRANCE 98

WORLD CUP

© 1994 ISL TM

OFFICIAL LICENSED PRODUCT

Keir Radnedge

CARLTON

(Above) The world's best: Brazil's Ronaldo is a goal-scoring machine

(Right) Lull before the storm: Stade de France is the venue for the final

This edition published 1998
by Carlton Books, 20 St Anne's Court,
Wardour Street, London W1V 3AW

Text and design copyright © 1998 Carlton Books Limited

Manufactured under licence by Carlton Books
© The France 98 Emblem and Official Mascot are copyrights and trademarks of ISL
© The Official World Cup FIFA Trophy is a copyright and a trademark of FIFA

Fabriqué sous licence par Carlton Books
© L'Emblème France 98 et la Mascotte Officielle sont des droits réservés d'ISL
© Le Trophée Officiel de la Coupe du Monde FIFA est une marque de la FIFA

A CIP record for this book is available from the British Library

ISBN 1 85868 441 2

The publishers would like to thank the following sources for their kind permission to reproduce the pictures in this book: AP Photo/Michel Lipchitz; Allsport UK Ltd./Shaun Botterill, Clive Brunskill, David cannon, Stu Forster, David Leah, Gary M Prior, Ben Radford, Mark Thompson, Vandystadt/Frederic Nebinger; Colorsport; Mark Leech; Popperfoto, Professional Sport; Sporting Pictures(uk)Ltd.
Every effort has been made to acknowledge correctly and contact the source and/or copyright holder of each picture, and Carlton Books Limited apologises for any unintentional errors or omissions which will be corrected in future editions of this book.

Introduction

Great players creating, saving and scoring great goa provide the World Cup with its drama.

No event in the football calendar is more eager awaited than the four-yearly extravaganza — ar France 98 will be bigger and better than ever.

This time 32 finalists compete compared with 24 the United States four years ago. That means bigger stage on which more outstanding players cc display their talent.

Great names shine down the years since tl inaugural World Cup in Uruguay in 1930. The fir was Frenchman Lucien Laurent who scored the firs ever World Cup goal. Later came the likes of Brazil Leonidas, Austria's Matthias Sindelar and Italy Giuseppe Meazza.

After the war the great players flooded throug the World Cup gates. Brazil gave the game Ademi Didi, Garrincha, Zico, Socrates and the incomparab Pele. England responded with Bobby Moore ar Bobby Charlton, Germany with Franz Beckenbaue Holland with Johan Cruyff.

Now a fresh generation takes the stage. Ronaldo the new hero of Brazil, a teenage spectator fror 1994 who has exploded to superstardom in a fe short years. Argentina offer Ariel Ortega as heir the fabulous talent of Diego Maradona, England loo to the goal-hunger of Alan Shearer and Germany Jürgen Klinsmann bids to achieve the "double" European champions and World Cup holders.

When it's all over only one country can boa possession of the World Cup. But all these supersta and more will have thrilled the world along the way.

Contents

Gabriel BATISTUTA
ARGENTINA

BORN: February 1, 1969
CLUBS: Newell's Old Boys, River Plate, Boca Juniors, Fiorentina (Italy)
POSITION/STYLE OF PLAY: Centre-forward/courageous, direct with fierce, instantaneous shot
INTERNATIONAL CAREER: 54 caps (36 goals)
FRANCE '98 QUALIFYING RECORD: 7 games/3 goals

It was bad news for Argentina's World Cup finals rivals when coach Daniel Passarella announced that Gabriel Batistuta would be leading their attack in France. The two men had fallen out during the latter stages of the qualifying competition and it was thought that the man nicknamed "Batigol" by his adoring fans in Florence might be overlooked. No chance. If Passarella needed proof that Batistuta was "up" for the World Cup, he would have acquired it merely by watching the centre-forward's hungry, two-goal display for the Rest of the World in the all-star match which preceded the World Cup draw in Marseille in December. Batistuta, who led Argentina's attack at the 1994 finals in the United States, is one of the few players to have played for both Argentine giants Boca Juniors and River Plate. He moved to Italy with Fiorentina in 1991 and was the top scorer in Serie A with 26 goals in 1994–95. He has totalled more than 130 goals in league, cup and European competition for Fiorentina.

Dennis BERGKAMP
HOLLAND

BORN: May 10, 1969
CLUBS: Wilskracht SNL (Amsterdam), Ajax, Internazionale (Italy), Arsenal (England)
POSITION/STYLE OF PLAY: Central midfield or forward/as forceful on the pitch as he is shy off it
INTERNATIONAL CAREER: 55 caps (33 goals)
FRANCE '98 QUALIFYING RECORD: 6 games/6 goals

Bergkamp, considered one of the world's top four players in FIFA's latest Footballer of the Year poll, was named after his father's own football hero – Scotland's sixties' star Denis Law. He was more than fulfilling all expectations when still a teenager he made his league debut for Ajax at 17 in a 2–0 home win against Roda in December 1986. While still a student that same season, Bergkamp helped Ajax win the 1986–87 Cup-winners Cup. In 1990, he was voted Dutch Young Player of the Year and was soon rushed up through the youth, under-21 and B international ranks. In 1992 Bergkamp was the star of the show as Ajax won both the Dutch league and UEFA Cup. Internazionale beat off several other clubs to secure his transfer and he won the UEFA Cup again with them in 1994. However Bergkamp was ill at ease in Italian football and transferred to Arsenal – with whom he has regained all his zest for the game – in 1995. He made his international debut against Italy in 1990 and helped Holland reach the quarter-finals of the 1994 World Cup.

5

Jorge CAMPOS
MEXICO

BORN: October 15, 1966

CLUBS: UNAM, Atlante, Cruz Azul, Los Angeles Galaxy (United States)

POSITION/STYLE OF PLAY: Goalkeeper-sweeper/often found closer to the halfway line than his own goal line

INTERNATIONAL CAREER: 55 caps (3 goals)

FRANCE '98 QUALIFYING RECORD: 8 games/0 goals

Campos is the most colourful figure in world football thanks to the famously flamboyant goalkeeping outfits which have dazzled fans in both Mexico and the United States where he plays Major League Soccer for Los Angeles Galaxy. Indeed, Campos claims he got the ideas for his idiosyncratic style of dress from his other love — surfing down the rolling ocean waves on the beaches at Acapulco on Mexico's south coast. Campos has been one of the inspirations of Mexico's 1990s revival — sparked by their performance in the 1993 Copa America in Ecuador where Mexico competed as guests and finished runners-up. Afterwards the one-time Argentina coach, Cesar Luis Menotti, described Campos as "a goalkeeper of the 21st century." Menotti had special knowledge of Campos since, as boss of Mexico between January 1991 and December 1992, he had brought Campos into the national team — ignoring critics who claimed that Campos was far too adventurous to be an international keeper. An outstanding forward when not selected in goal, Campos often stands way beyond his penalty area when his team are attacking but claims it's a style which has saved many more goals than it has cost.

John COLLINS
SCOTLAND

BORN: January 31, 1968
CLUBS: Hibernian, Celtic, Monaco
 (France)
POSITION/STYLE OF PLAY:
 Midfield/long or short passes all
 delivered with equal accuracy
INTERNATIONAL CAREER: 46 caps
 (9 goals)
FRANCE '98 QUALIFYING RECORD:
 8 games/1 goal

Scotland manager Craig Brown believes that Collins, with his intimate knowledge of French football, language and lifestyle, could prove to be their secret weapon at the World Cup finals. Yet Collins's home town of Galashiels in the Scottish borders is more renowned for producing rugby players. He chose the other code with instant success and made his Scottish league debut for Hibernian against Aberdeen in 1985. Three years later he scored on his debut for Scotland against Saudi Arabia. Two more years and Hibernian could hold out no longer — selling Collins to Celtic for £900,000. Renowned for his "dead ball" striking ability, he was the only Scottish player to appear in all his country's qualifying matches in the 1996 European Championship. He was a subject of controversy after the finals, however, when he took advantage of the Bosman Judgement to move from Celtic to Monaco on the expiry of his contract without a fee being due. Celtic subsequently failed in a bid to challenge the move, claiming in vain that Monte Carlo is not a European Union state.

Frank de BOER
HOLLAND

BORN: May 15, 1970
CLUB: Ajax Amsterdam
POSITION/STYLE OF PLAY: Central defender/never happier than when advancing for a header or free kick on the rival goal
INTERNATIONAL CAREER: 50 caps (5 goals)
FRANCE '98 QUALIFYING RECORD: 7 games/4 goals

Frank De Boer is now the key man at the heart of the Dutch defence following the national team retirements in the past couple of years of first Ronald Koeman and then De Boer's Ajax team-mate, Danny Blind. De Boer, whose twin brother Ronald has shared most of his success with both Ajax and the Dutch national team, helped Holland reach the semi-finals of the 1992 European Championship but was sadly missed because of injury at the 1996 finals. Dutch experts insist that their favourites would not have fallen apart against England at Wembley had De Boer been in place to seal up the centre of defence. De Boer had made nearly 400 appearances for Ajax in league, cup and European competition – first achieving international attention as a member of the Ajax side which beat Torino of Italy on the away goals rule to win the 1991–92 UEFA Cup. In the past two years he has not only taken over from Koeman as a defensive bulwark in the Dutch side, but has developed his own reputation as a free kick specialist – and contributed three of Holland's 10 goals against San Marino in the World Cup qualifying competition.

Marcel DESAILLY
FRANCE

BORN: September 7, 1968
CLUBS: Nantes, Marseille, AC Milan (Italy)
POSITION/STYLE OF PLAY: Midfield/tough-guy tackling style means he is equally at home in central defence
INTERNATIONAL CAREER: 37 caps (1 goal)
1997 RECORD: 7 games/0 goals

Desailly, the Ghana-born midfielder or defender, holds a place in world football history as the first man to have won the European Champions Cup with two different clubs in successive seasons — with Marseille against Milan in 1993 and then with Milan against Barcelona a year later. Desailly moved to France with his family at the age of four and made his name initially with local club Nantes. His power and versatility were soon appreciated elsewhere and in 1992 Desailly was sold to Marseille with whom he won the league title and then, in 1993, the Champions Cup — marking Milan's Marco Van Basten out of the game. But disaster was around the corner for Marseille. Two weeks after the European triumph, the club were plunged into a match-fixing scandal and subsequent financial disaster. All their star players had to be sold to pay the club's debts. Desailly was an obvious target for a string of clubs but it was Milan, remembering Desailly's starring role against Van Basten, who snapped him up. They have no regrets. After helping them win the Italian league and Champions Cup in 1994, Desailly collected another Serie A title in 1996.

Didier DESCHAMPS
FRANCE

BORN: October 15, 1968

CLUBS: Bayonne, Nantes, Bordeaux, Marseille, Juventus (Italy)

POSITION/STYLE OF PLAY: Midfield/small in stature but huge in tenacity and influence

INTERNATIONAL CAREER: 63 caps (4 goals)

1997 RECORD: 6 games/1 goal

Deschamps has been the cornerstone of the French international midfield for most of the 1990s — his tight control and accurate distribution of the ball making him a magnet for team-mates both with France and his Italian club, Juventus, as they build attack after attack. Deschamps, who first played for France against Yugoslavia in 1989, made his top division debut in August 1986. He won French league championship medals with Marseille in 1990 and 1992 and the Italian championship with Juventus in 1995. In 1993, he captained the Marseille team who won the European Champions Cup in Munich against Milan. In his first season with Juventus, whom he joined in July 1994, he won the Italian league and cup as well as finishing runner-up in the UEFA Cup. He won the European Champions Cup again in 1995–96 with Juventus, after which he also helped steer France to the semi-finals of the European Championship in England. His 46th cap earned in a friendly against Portugal in January of 1996 took him into the top 20 of most-capped French players.

Youri DJORKAEFF
FRANCE

BORN: March 9, 1968
CLUBS: Grenoble, Strasbourg, Monaco, Paris Saint-Germain, Internazionale (Italy)
POSITION/STYLE OF PLAY:
Midfield/endless stamina enables him to operate as both midfielder and forward simultaneously
INTERNATIONAL CAREER: 31 caps (17 goals)
1997 RECORD: 6 games/3 goals

Djorkaeff has followed in his father Jean's footsteps as a high-profile international footballer. He grew up with a string of provincial clubs before making his name as a youthful member of the Monaco side who reached the 1992 Cup-winners Cup Final before losing to Werder Bremen. The following season he underlined his growing reputation by finishing as top scorer in the French top division with 20 goals. In June 1995 he moved on up the ladder by signing for Paris Saint-Germain – exactly 25 years to the day after his father, who played fullback for France at the 1966 World Cup finals in England, had done so. Djorkaeff made his senior national team debut for France in 1993 against Israel. In 1995, the sports newspaper *L'Equipe* named him Footballer of the Year. Barely five months later he was PSG's star in their victory over Rapid Vienna in the Cup-winners Cup Final in Belgium. That was virtually his last game for the Parisian club since he joined Internazionale a few weeks later – after first starring for the French team who reached the semi-finals of the 1996 European Championship.

Gheorghe HAGI
ROMANIA

BORN: February 5, 1965

POSITION/STYLE OF PLAY:
Midfield/playmaker who is the fulcrum of the Romanian game

CLUBS: Constanta, Sportul Studentesc, Steaua, Real Madrid (Spain), Brescia (Italy), Barcelona (Spain), Galatasaray (Turkey)

INTERNATIONAL CAREER: 107 caps (32 goals)

FRANCE '98 QUALIFYING RECORD:
6 games/5 goals

The 1998 World Cup finals will be the pinnacle of Hagi's career since Romania's midfield general intends to retire from international football this summer – 17 years after he made his top division debut as a 16-year-old for Constanta. At 18 he was making his international debut in a World Cup qualifying match against East Germany and, by the age of 21 Hagi, with Sportul, was top scorer in the Romanian league. At the insistence of the ruling Ceausescu family, Hagi then left Sportul to play for their favourite team Steaua. He was a league and cup double-winner three times in a row before moving to Real Madrid after guiding Romania to the second round of the 1990 World Cup finals. Two years later, he was signed by Italy's Brescia before moving again – after starring for Romania at the 1994 World Cup finals – to Barcelona. Spanish football, however, never quite suited Hagi and he regained his old form after moving closer to home with Turkey's Galatasaray. By now he had become only the second Romanian after Ladislau Boloni to win more than 100 caps.

Victor **IKPEBA**
NIGERIA

BORN: June 12, 1973
CLUBS: FC Liege (Belgium), Monaco (France)
POSITION: Midfield/roaming schemer who considers the entire breadth of midfield to come under his control
INTERNATIONAL CAREER: 14 caps (3 goals)
FRANCE '98 QUALIFYING RECORD: 4 games/0 goals

Nigeria's national team has been overflowing with outstanding midfielders but Monaco's Ikpeba promises to be the finest of all. His talent, youthful achievement and ongoing potential were recognized in December 1997 when Ikpeba was voted African Footballer of the Year by the African Football Confederation. Yet Ikpeba never played football professionally in his homeland. Instead he honed his skills on the streets of the Lagos suburb of Yaba and had played only one teenage season as a teenage amateur when he was included in the Nigerian squad for the 1989 World Junior Cup in Scotland. After the finals he moved to Europe with Belgian club FC Liege, scoring 27 goals in 89 league games in four seasons. In 1992–93 he was voted Young Player of the Year in Belgium, earning a transfer to Monaco with whom he made an enormous impact in the 1993–94 UEFA Champions League. In the summer of 1994 Ikpeba was a non-playing reserve in Nigeria's squad as they reached their first ever World Cup finals but two years later he starred in their gold-medal-winning team at the Atlanta Olympics.

Kasey KELLER
USA

BORN: January 27, 1969
CLUBS: Portland University, Millwall (England), Leicester City (England)
POSITION/STYLE OF PLAY:
Goalkeeper/agility and sharp reflexes matched with apparently elastic arms
INTERNATIONAL CAREER: 25 caps (0 goals)
FRANCE '98 QUALIFYING RECORD:
9 games/0 goals

Kasey Keller was out of the picture when the United States were World Cup hosts in 1994. But coach Steve Sampson is not making that mistake this time. Nor can fans doubt the goalkeeper's commitment to the cause after computing the thousands of air miles he has totted up as a transatlantic commuter in helping secure the US their third successive finals appearance. But Keller has always enjoyed keeping busy — when he moved to English football originally with Millwall he also managed, through a correspondence course, to complete his graduation in sociology from Portland University, Oregon. Maintaining such dedication saw Keller duly rewarded with the captaincy of Team America at the 1996 Olympic Games and a runners-up placing in the 1997 US Player of the Year awards. Keller also collected a League Cup-winner's medal back in England as Leicester City defeated Middlesbrough in a replayed Final. Yet Keller nearly missed out on a Leicester move. On leaving Millwall he appeared bound for Germany with Kaiserslautern or Leverkusen until Leicester came in at the last minute with a decisive £900,000 bid. It's proved to be money well spent.

Jürgen KLINSMANN
GERMANY

BORN: July 30, 1964

CLUBS: Gingen, Geislingen, Stuttgart Kickers, VfB Stuttgart, Internazionale (Italy), Monaco (France), Tottenham Hotspur (England), Bayern Munich, Sampdoria (Italy), Tottenham (England)

POSITION/STYLE OF PLAY: Forward/lanky, all-action attacker whose goal-hungry ambitions have prevented ever considering the usual veteran's move back into midfield

INTERNATIONAL CAREER: 100 caps (43 goals)

FRANCE '98 QUALIFYING RECORD: 9 games/3 goals

Germany's captain will wind up his national team career at the World Cup finals. But he will do so intending to go out right at the top – having added the honour of lifting the World Cup to the delight of captaining Germany to European Championship victory two years ago. Few players are more internationally-qualified since Klinsmann has played professional football in four countries – Germany, Italy (two spells), France and England (two spells). The adventure began a decade ago when "Klinsi" was 19-goal top scorer in the German league and made his international debut against Brazil. In 1990 he won the World Cup and stayed on in Italy with Internazionale, with whom he won the UEFA Cup in 1991 before joining Monaco. Twice Klinsmann was voted Footballer of the Year in Germany (in 1988 and 1994) and he was acclaimed as Footballer of the Year in England in 1995, on the strength of a remarkable season with Tottenham. Back home with Bayern Munich, Klinsmann scored a record 15 goals on their way to another UEFA Cup success before taking off yet again – first for Sampdoria then back to Tottenham.

Brian **LAUDRUP**
DENMARK

BORN: February 22, 1969

CLUBS: Brondby, Bayer Urdingen (Germany), Bayern Munich (Germany), Fiorentina (Italy), Milan (Italy), Rangers (Scotland)

POSITION/STYLE OF PLAY:
Forward/mixes the pace of a winger with the vision of a playmaker and the accurate shooting of a top-class striker

INTERNATIONAL CAREER: 73 caps (18 goals)

FRANCE '98 QUALIFYING RECORD:
7 games/4 goals

Brian Laudrup, the younger brother of Michael and son of former Danish international Finn, has lost nothing by comparison with his relatives. He made his international debut at 18 against Germany in 1987, won the Danish Cup with Brondby in 1989 and starred in Denmark's astonishing European Championship triumph in 1992. Bayer Urdingen took Laudrup to Germany but he soon moved on for a domestic record fee to Bayern Munich before following brother Michael's example and trying his luck in Italy. The Fiorentina fans loved Laudrup but his transfer to Milan turned sour because the club had more foreigners than they needed and he spent more games on the subs' bench or in the stand than on the pitch. It took a surprise move to Scotland with Rangers to reignite Laudrup's enthusiasm for the game. Twice he was voted Scottish Footballer of the Year — the first foreigner to win the award — as Rangers set about matching Celtic's record of nine championships in a row. Laudrup was also Player of the Year a record three times in Denmark, in 1989, 1992 and 1995.

Paolo MALDINI
ITALY

BORN: June 26, 1968
CLUB: Milan
POSITION/STYLE OF PLAY: Leftback or sweeper/perfect timing in the tackle, great control, pace, accurate shot on overlapping in attack
INTERNATIONAL CAREER: 85 caps (5 goals)
FRANCE '98 QUALIFYING RECORD: 10 games/2 goals

Paolo Maldini, proud captain of Italy and the son of Cesare Maldini who is the country's national coach, is more than just one of the world's top defenders: he is one of the game's finest all-round footballers. When Italy finished second in the 1994 World Cup, all the critics present in the United States agreed that Maldini's duel with Brazil's Cafu was a highlight of the Final – and World Soccer magazine duly voted him its World Player of the Year for 1994. Father Cesare was a star sweeper with Milan in the early 1960s and has been thrilled to see Paolo emulate his own achievements as an international footballer and, more specifically, a European Champions Cup-winner. Maldini junior did not have an easy time because of his family connections, however. He says: "If anything, my father worked me harder than the rest of the Milan youth team, just so no-one could ever accuse him of favouritism." Paolo is leaner, taller and quicker than Cesare was and just as sharp at reading the game. Now he will captain his country at the World Cup finals – something his father never achieved during his own career.

17

Ariel ORTEGA
ARGENTINA

BORN: April 3, 1974
CLUBS: General Martin, River Plate,
    Valencia (Spain)
POSITION/STYLE OF PLAY:
    Midfield/livewire orchestrator of
    attack with nimble footwork and an
    Olympic sprinter's acceleration
INTERNATIONAL CAREER: 42 caps
    (7 goals)
FRANCE '98 QUALIFYING RECORD:
    15 games/4 goals

Ariel Ortega never wanted to be anything other than a footballer. He played for local youth teams in Jujuy and then, at 15, was spotted by River Plate, one of the greatest clubs in Argentina. Ortega counted River's Europe-bound winger Claudio Caniggia as one of his heroes and was signed as his successor. Coach Daniel Passarella – now national boss – feared the new boy might prove too small and lightweight but not only did Ortega make an instant impression on Passarella and River Plate's fans but he also caught the eye of then national coach Alfio Basile. His national team debut duly followed in a 3–1 win over Morocco in April 1994. That earned Ortega a place in the World Cup squad. He was expected to be a non-playing reserve. But then Diego Maradona failed a dope test and Caniggia was injured midway through the first half of the key group match against Bulgaria. Basile gambled on substitute Ortega – and that gamble proved his springboard to World Cup fame, international acclaim and, in due course, a lucrative transfer to Spain's Valencia. This time Ortega approaches the World Cup as a star in his own right.

RAUL

BORN: June 27, 1977
CLUBS: Atletico Madrid, Real Madrid
POSITION/STYLE OF PLAY:
Forward/pace, close control and sharp
shot means he makes chances as easily
as he takes them
INTERNATIONAL CAREER: 10 caps
(1 goal)
FRANCE '98 QUALIFYING RECORD:
9 games/1 goal

Raul Gonzalez Blanco — known simply as Raul to Spanish fans — is proof that, even in the post-Bosman football world, home-town loyalty still counts for plenty. Real Madrid's new hero is the son of an electrician from a working-class suburb of the Spanish capital. Yet he was given away as a teenager by neighbours Atletico when they scrapped their youth section to save money. Real have been grateful ever since — so has Raul, especially since signing a new multi-million-dollar contract. It was Argentine coach Jorge Valdano who took the gamble on throwing Raul, then just 18, in at the deep end. But starring displays against Barcelona and — ironically — Atletico Madrid justified Valdano's faith and drew an £8 million bid from Italian club Roma. Spanish fans were horrified when national boss Javier Clemente decided to leave Raul at home for the 1996 European Championship finals — and still believe his eye for a half-chance could have proved crucial in the quarter-final against England which Spain lost on penalties. Raul has been a regular ever since!

BRAZIL ROMARIO

BORN: January 29, 1966
CLUBS: Vasco da Gama, PSV Eindhoven (Holland), Barcelona (Spain), Flamengo, Valencia (Spain), Flamengo
POSITION/STYLE OF PLAY: Centre-forward/perfect control means he can receive passes and create danger despite having being encircled by defenders
INTERNATIONAL CAREER: 56 caps (42 goals)
1997 RECORD: 17 games/20 goals

Romario de Souza Faria: the poor boy who learned his football in the streets of Rio de Janeiro is acknowledged as one of the best players of this decade. He began with Vasco da Gama and starred in the Brazilian team who won the silver medal at the 1988 Olympic Games in Seoul. Romario then conquered Europe playing for PSV Eindhoven and Barcelona, but his volatile temper and youthful exuberance restricted his appearances for the senior Brazil national team. He was recalled finally in 1993 when Brazil needed to beat Uruguay to qualify for the World Cup finals and he scored the two decisive goals. The following year Romario was voted top player as he inspired Brazil to win the Cup for a historic fourth time. Romario was growing increasingly homesick in Europe so, in the spring of 1995, Barcelona transferred him home to Flamengo. Romario's exotic lifestyle earned as many headlines as his goals but when Flamengo hit financial trouble Romario had to be sold back to Europe, to Valencia. The move soon turned sour but at least Romario regained his place in Brazil's attack — and his partnership with Ronaldo should terrorize opposing defences during the forthcoming World Cup.

BRAZIL RONALDO

BORN: September 22, 1976
CLUBS: Cruzeiro, PSV Eindhoven, Barcelona (Spain), Internazionale (Italy)
POSITION/STYLE OF PLAY: Centre-forward/the complete player — possessing every possible talent on the ground, in the air, in the penalty box and out of it
INTERNATIONAL CAREER: 29 caps (20 goals)
1997 RECORD: 20 games/15 goals

Ronaldo Luiz Nazario de Lima is the world's most talked-about footballer. He won the FIFA Footballer of the Year award twice in succession in 1996 and 1997 and last summer moved to Italian club Internazionale of Milan for a world record £19.5 million. Ronaldo was born in Rio de Janeiro in 1976 and his talent was first spotted by former World Cup hero Jairzinho. In his first season with Cruzeiro, Ronaldo scored 54 goals. Dutch club PSV Eindhoven heard the news, snapped him up, then sold him on to Barcelona for nearly £13 million. Ronaldo was the Spanish league's top scorer that season with 34 goals and also converted the penalty which won Barcelona the European Cup-winners-Cup. Brazil national coach Carlos Alberto Parreira took him to USA '94 as a member of the World Cup-winning side, but at only 17 years old Ronaldo was there only to gain experience and did not play. However, in the four years since then, he has established himself as the greatest player in the world and the man on whom Brazil will rely to secure a record fifth World Cup success.

Matthias SAMMER
GERMANY

BORN: September 5, 1967

CLUBS: Grödlitz, Einheit Dresden, Dynamo Dresden, Stuttgart, Internazionale (Italy), Borussia Dortmund (Germany)

POSITION/STYLE OF PLAY: Sweeper/superior control for a centre-back means he can turn defence into attack like a modern Beckenbauer

INTERNATIONAL CAREER: 51 caps (23 for former East Germany) and eight goals (six for former East Germany)

FRANCE '98 QUALIFYING RECORD: 3 games/0 goals

Sammer, son of a former Dynamo Dresden and East German international midfielder, made his international debut for the unified Germany in 1990 against Switzerland – having already built his reputation with the former German Democratic Republic. The young Sammer twice became an East Germany league championship winner with Dresden in 1989 and 1990. Also in 1990, he was an East German cup-winner before becoming one of the first GDR stars to transfer to the West with Stuttgart. Sammer was German champion with Stuttgart in 1992 and with Borussia Dortmund in 1995 and 1996. In between he spent half a season in Italy with Internazionale in 1993 but failed to adjust to the lifestyle or football. Sammer's absence through injury from the 1994 World Cup quarter-final against Bulgaria was considered a contributory factor to the Germans' defeat. Conversely, his presence at Euro 96 was a key element in Germany's title triumph. A year later he also starred in Borussia Dortmund's Champions Cup victory over Juventus.

Peter SCHMEICHEL
DENMARK

BORN: November 18, 1963
CLUBS: Gladsaxe Hero, Hvidovre, Brondby, Manchester United (England)
POSITION/STYLE OF PLAY: Goalkeeper/big man who appears to fill the entire goalmouth and is never afraid to order his team-mates around
INTERNATIONAL CAREER: 97 caps (0 goals)
FRANCE '98 QUALIFYING RECORD: 8 games/0 goals

Schmeichel, a regular contender for the annual world's top goalkeeper award, began his professional life running a charity shop part-time for the World Wildlife Fund. He was also, briefly, a newspaper advertising salesman before his £750,000 move to Manchester United in 1991. He had already been an international for four years, having made his debut against Greece in 1987 and then came to prominence in the 1988 European Championship finals when he replaced Troels Rasmussen in the Danes' final first round group match against Italy. Schmeichel was voted Footballer of the Year in Denmark in both 1990 and 1993 and, in between, he was one of the inspirations of the national team's astonishing success in the 1992 European Championship — above all in the penalty shoot-out victory over Holland in the semi-finals. Schmeichel has been a key figure in Manchester United's historic "double Double" era of the 1990s — his all-action style even bringing him a rare goalkeeper's goal when he dashed upfield in the closing stages of a European tie against Rotor Volgograd.

David SEAMAN
ENGLAND

BORN: September 19, 1963

CLUBS: Leeds United, Peterborough United, Birmingham City, Queens Park Rangers, Arsenal

POSITION/STYLE OF PLAY:
Goalkeeper/exudes confidence with an all-enveloping style which gives him an added advantage in penalty shoot-outs

INTERNATIONAL CAREER: 38 caps (0 goals)

FRANCE '98 QUALIFYING RECORD: 7 games/0 goals

Seaman was a late developer whose career did not fully "take off" until after he moved across London from QPR to join Arsenal in May 1990 for a reported £1.3 million — then a record fee for an English goalkeeper. Seaman took over at Highbury from John Lukic, who went to Leeds — where Seaman had spent a year as a teenager without playing in the first team. With Arsenal he has won four medals in four competitions: one each for the league championship, FA Cup, Coca-Cola League Cup and European Cup-winners Cup. It might have been two European medals but Seaman unluckily finished on the losing side when Arsenal lost in the last minute of extra time to Zaragoza in the 1995 Cup-winners Cup Final. If the tie had gone to extra-time Seaman's prowess in the penalty shoot-out department might well have seen Arsenal through. Seaman has been first-choice for England for the past six seasons after having had to wait patiently in line behind Peter Shilton and Chris Woods. Seaman made his international debut in 1988 against Saudi Arabia, and now boasts almost 800 senior appearances in international and domestic competition.

Alan SHEARER
ENGLAND

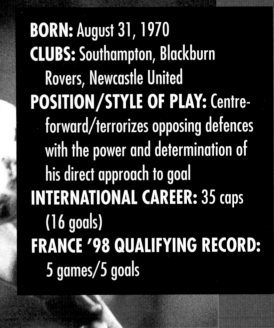

BORN: August 31, 1970
CLUBS: Southampton, Blackburn Rovers, Newcastle United
POSITION/STYLE OF PLAY: Centre-forward/terrorizes opposing defences with the power and determination of his direct approach to goal
INTERNATIONAL CAREER: 35 caps (16 goals)
FRANCE '98 QUALIFYING RECORD: 5 games/5 goals

Shearer, a Geordie spirited away by Southampton in 1988, should be one of the hungriest attackers at the World Cup finals — after having to miss virtually all the first half of the season because of injury. The career which led to Shearer's appointment as England captain began in sensational style when, at the tender age of 17 years and 240 days, he scored a hat-trick against Arsenal, in only his fourth senior appearance. He thus established a place in the record books as the youngest player ever to hit a Football League hat-trick. Southampton could not afford to hang on to Shearer and he was transferred to Blackburn Rovers in July 1992 for a domestic record £3.3 million. Rovers' reward on their investment was to see Shearer hit 34 goals in 1994–95 to inspire Blackburn's first modern league championship. In due course he went on to become the first man to score 100 goals in the Premiership before he was sold to Newcastle — home, at last! — for a then world record £13 million. Shearer was voted Footballer of the Year in 1994 and Players' Player of the Year in 1997.

Hristo STOICHKOV
BULGARIA

BORN: February 8, 1966

CLUBS: Maritza Plovdiv, Hebros Harmanli, CSKA Sofia, Barcelona (Spain), Parma (Italy), Barcelona (Spain)

POSITION/STYLE OF PLAY: Forward/pretends to direct operations from wide on the left then sneaks in for a decisive crack at goal

INTERNATIONAL CAREER: 68 caps (35 goals)

FRANCE '98 QUALIFYING RECORD: 4 games/1 goal

Stoichkov is a moody, brooding talent – but also the greatest player ever to come out of Bulgaria for whom he has been scoring goals ever since a 3–2 win over the United Arab Emirates in Dubai in 1988. Voted Footballer of the Year in Bulgaria for four successive years from 1989 to 1992, he was three times league champion in Bulgaria with CSKA. Stoichkov was then voted European Footballer of the Year in 1994 after being runner-up in 1992. He was also joint winner of the 1989–90 Golden Boot as top league scorer in Europe with 38 goals. Barcelona signed him from CSKA on coach Johan Cruyff's personal recommendation and for four successive seasons from 1991–1994 he helped inspire their Spanish championship successes. In 1992 Stoichkov helped Barça achieve their most desperately-demanded success when they won the European Champions Cup. Two more years and he was on top of the world as joint top scorer at the 1994 World Cup when Bulgaria finished fourth. Stoichkov fell out with his own federation after Bulgaria flopped at the 1996 European Championship but they all shook hands and made up midway through the successful 1998 World Cup qualifying campaign.

Davor SUKER
CROATIA

BORN: January 1, 1968
CLUBS: Osijek, FC Croatia Zagreb, Sevilla (Spain), Real Madrid (Spain)
POSITION/STYLE OF PLAY: Centre-forward/stylish attack leader with deceptively ruthless touch in front of goal
INTERNATIONAL CAREER: 32 caps (2 for the former Yugoslavia) and 26 goals (1 for the former Yugoslavia)
FRANCE '98 QUALIFYING RECORD: 9 games/5 goals

Suker has been a prize-winning star ever since, as a teenager, he was a member of the former Yugoslavia squad which won the World Youth Cup in Chile in 1987. Three years later Suker made his international debut against Romania. He was also a non-playing member of the Slav squad which reached the quarter-finals of the 1990 World Cup. But he accrued only one more appearance before the former Yugoslavia was split apart and he could play for his "real" homeland of Croatia. Top league goalscorer with 18 goal for Osijek in the former Yugoslavia, Suker was brought out to Western Europe by Sevilla of Spain and then transferred on to Real Madrid after starring at the finals of the 1996 European Championship in England. Croatia reached the quarter-finals and Suker scored perhaps the Goal of the Tournament when he chipped Peter Schmeichel in a first-round victory over Denmark. A leading influence within the national squad, Suker is the star player with the business brain who negotiates his team's play and conditions with the federation and potential sponsors.

Carlos VALDERRAMA
COLUMBIA

BORN: September 2, 1961

CLUBS: Santa Marta, Millonarios, Atletico Nacional, Montpellier (France), Valladolid (Spain), Medellin, Atletico Junior Barranquilla, Tampa Bay (United States), Miami Fusion (United States)

POSITION/STYLE OF PLAY: Midfield/playmaker who is always available for passes out of defence or going forward in attack

INTERNATIONAL CAREER: 103 caps (9 goals)

FRANCE '98 QUALIFYING RECORD: 15 games/3 goals

Valderrama, despite having twice retired from international football, is hoping to make it third time lucky at the 1998 World Cup finals. The frizzy-haired midfielder was the key man in the Colombian side who lost in extra-time to Cameroon in the second round of the finals in Italy in 1990 and then crashed out in the first round in the United States, amid controversy and tragedy, four years later. Valderrama first made his name at the 1987 Copa America when he inspired Colombia's third-place finish and thus earned the South American Footballer of the Year accolade – which he regained in 1993. He moved to France with Montpellier then went to Spain with Valladolid but failed to impress in Europe. As soon as he had returned to Colombian football, however, he rediscovered all his old zest for the game. Last year he not only proved outstanding in the long drawn-out South American section of the World Cup qualifying tournament but achieved the honour of becoming the first Colombian footballer to top a century of caps for his country.

Ivan ZAMORANO

BORN: January 18, 1967

CLUBS: Cobresal, Bologna (Italy), St Gallen (Switzerland), Sevilla (Spain), Real Madrid (Spain), Internazionale (Italy)

POSITION/STYLE OF PLAY: Centre-forward/wiry, pacy attack leader who likes nothing better than to arrow through the heart of opposing defences

INTERNATIONAL CAREER: 37 caps (23 goals)

FRANCE '98 QUALIFYING RECORD: 10 games/12 goals

Zamorano considers the 1998 World Cup finals as the natural progression in a career which has taken him steadily up the soccer ladder. He came to Europe originally a decade ago for a trial with Italy's Bologna which did not work out. Zamorano was then given a trial by St Gallen in Switzerland and impressed so much that he was snapped up by Sevilla of Spain. From there he moved onto Real Madrid. Coach Jorge Valdano expressed public doubts over whether Zamorano had the necessary talent and temperament but the Chilean provided the ideal answer — scoring the 28 goals which did not lead Madrid to the 1994–95 Spanish league championship but saw him honoured as the league's top marksman. Zamorano stayed with Madrid despite intense speculation over a possible move to Borussia Dortmund but finally moved on in 1996, joining Internazionale of Italy. He was disappointed when Inter dropped him in favour of Brazil's Ronaldo in 1997 but found consolation by scoring a remarkable 12 goals in 10 games for Chile in the World Cup qualifying competition. His partnership with Marcello Salas tore apart the best defences in South America.

Zinedine ZIDANE
FRANCE

BORN: June 23, 1972

CLUBS: Cannes, Bordeaux, Juventus (Italy)

POSITION/STYLE OF PLAY: Midfield/puts in an enormous amount of hard work to make the best use of his technical skills

International career: 28 caps (6 goals)

1997 RECORD: 8 games/1 goal

Zinedine Zidane's status as the most popular footballer in France was underlined when the hosts nominated him as their representative to play for Europe in the all-star match against the Rest of the World which served as curtain-raiser to the World Cup draw in Marseille last December. Zidane shot to superstardom after having made his top division debut in May 1989 and joining Bordeaux in 1992. Two years later he was voted Best Young Player in France and duly scored both France's goals to salvage a 2–2 draw on his international debut against the Czech Republic in the same year. Zidane's finest domestic season was 1995–96 when he played more games than any other player in the country – nearly 60 in league, cup, UEFA Cup and European Championship. He also won the 1995 French Goal of the Year award for a left-footed 35-metre lob which beat Betis of Spain in the UEFA Cup. The goal was shown on television around Europe and provoked interest from Juventus of Italy, whom Zidane joined in the summer of 1996. He's become the darling of the Turin fans who consider him the "new Platini" – after their French hero of the 1980s.

Gianfranco ZOLA
ITALY

BORN: July 5, 1966
CLUBS: Nuorese, Torres, Napoli, Parma, Chelsea (England)
POSITION/STYLE OF PLAY:
Forward/free-kick expert whose eye for the defence-splitting pass is matched by his talent for scoring goals from any distance
INTERNATIONAL CAREER: 35 caps (9 goals)
FRANCE '98 QUALIFYING RECORD:
8 games/2 goals

Most players would be overawed at stepping into the shoes of Diego Maradona at his greatest – but not Zola. In December 1989 the Sardinian kid rose to the challenge magnificently by scoring a wonderful 30-yard goal in a 3–1 win over Atalanta. One newspaper reported next morning: "Zola was so good, he even looked like Maradona." Once Maradona was fit again, Zola went back to the subs' bench. But he did not stay in the shadows for long and soon earned a regular place in Napoli's league title-winning side. His first cap for Italy followed in a European Championship qualifier against Norway before Zola moved on to Parma with whom he won the UEFA Cup. His first high-profile visit to England ended in ignominy when he missed a decisive penalty against Germany as Italy crashed out of the first round of the 1996 European Championship. But he returned in glory a few months later to sign for Chelsea, inspire them to FA Cup glory and collect the English Footballer of the Year prize. Scoring the goal which beat England at Wembley in a 1998 World Cup qualifier only served to underline that the little man has a great talent.

Andoni ZUBIZARRETA
SPAIN

BORN: October 23, 1961

CLUBS: Athletic Bilbao, Barcelona, Valencia

POSITION/STYLE OF PLAY: Goalkeeper/lanky, apparently awkward stance belies his command of defence, agility and safe hands

INTERNATIONAL CAREER: 121 caps (0 goals)

FRANCE '98 QUALIFYING RECORD: 10 games/0 goals

Zubizarreta is the goalkeeper who goes on and on... his career at the top now stretching back nearly 17 years since he made his league debut for Athletic Bilbao in September 1981. Four years later, in 1985, and "Zubi" was making his international debut as a second half substitute for Luis Arconada in a 3—1 win over Finland. Now he has the honour of being the only Spanish player to have earned more than 100 caps for his country — number 100 being secured in Spain's 2—0 win over Armenia in the last European Championship qualifying competition. Zubizarreta has been first-choice goalkeeper for Spain at the 1986, 1990 and 1994 World Cups and at the 1988 and 1996 European Championships. In 1986 he was sold from Bilbao to Barcelona for a then world record £1.6 million and went on to win four leagues titles, two cups, the European Champions Cup, Cup-winners Cup and European Supercup with Barcelona. Coach Johan Cruyff thought "Zubi" was past his best in 1994 and let him go to Valencia — but national boss Javier Clemente knew better and not only kept faith with Zubizarreta but installed him as national captain.